ESSO
ULME

SPORTS CLASSIC

THE GRAND PRIX

By JULIAN MAY

Creative Education
Childrens Press

PHOTO CREDITS:

UPI . . . . Cover, 1, 2, 6, 8, 11, 12, 14, 15, 17,
19, 21, 23, 24, 29, 31, 33, 35, 39, 43, 45, 48
AP 36, 41
Wide World 32

Published by Creative Educational Society, Inc., 123 South Broad Street, Mankato, Minnesota 56001. Printed in the United States.

Library of Congress Cataloging in Publication Data
May, Julian.
The Grand Prix world championship.
(Sports classic)
SUMMARY: Discusses the circuit leading to the World Championship of Driving and some of the victors in this world-wide, year-long race series.
1. Grand Prix racing—Juvenile literature. [1. Grand Prix racing. 2. Automobile racing—Biography] I. Title.
GV1029.M38 796.7'2'0922 [B] 76-5460 ISBN 0-87191-506-5

Contents

The U.S. leg of the Grand Prix circuit is run at Watkins Glen, N.Y.

World Championship of Driving

It is the biggest motor-racing challenge in the world. It demands the greatest skill of drivers and the greatest perfection of machines.

It is Grand Prix racing. Every year, its top-scoring driver is hailed as Champion of the World.

The words "Grand Prix" are French for "big prize." (If you aren't French, you can pronounce the words best by saying *grompree* very quickly.) The original Grand Prix race was run at Le Mans, France, back in 1906. It was won by a Hungarian with the speedy name of Szisz, who attained an average speed of 63 mph as he and his riding mechanic roared over the back roads of northwestern France.

Early auto races in Europe always took place on the public highways, and this tradition has continued to be a part of Grand Prix racing. Road racing produces a different breed of racing driver – unlike most of those familiar to American race fans. In the United States, motor racing mostly takes place on tracks. This is the reason why American drivers have always been fairly rare on the Grand Prix circuit, and why European drivers rarely compete in American races. Until very recently, not only the drivers but also the cars were so different that the two styles of racing could never mix.

The French started Grand Prix racing, but other nations were quick to compete. By the 1920's other

American driver Bruce Kessler escaped from this flaming wreck with minor injuries.

European countries had started their own Grands Prix.

The modern Grand Prix circuit leading to the World Championship of Driving began in 1950. The circuit included Grand Prix races in a number of countries – some run on blocked-off roads, others run on specially built courses that closely simulated public roadways.

The World Championship of Driving is awarded on a point basis. The first six finishers in a Grand Prix race are awarded the following points: First–9; Second–6; Third–4; Fourth–3; Fifth–2; Sixth–1.

The number of entries allowed in each Grand Prix race is carefully restricted. Because the cars are so expensive to build and maintain, only the most expert drivers can expect to get a chance to drive them.

Despite the "big prize" title, Grand Prix races offer mostly small prizes of money. The winners of these races reap rewards of a different sort – glory, hero-worship of millions of fans, and honors conferred by a grateful government or Queen. Wealthy jet-setters and "beautiful people" make pets of successful Grand Prix drivers. Then, too, if the driver is lucky, he may become a millionaire himself by endorsing different products.

If the driver is unlucky, all the glitter, excitement, and glory may only be a prelude to a flaming crash and death. Danger, as well as prestige, rides the Grand Prix racing circuit.

The Grand Prix circuit is spread over the year and over the globe. It progresses in rather definite steps, like the acts of a play, leading up to the climax that decides the World Champion.

In January the races are in South America, where it is summertime. First the Argentine, then the Brazilian Grands Prix serve as a kind of shakedown for crews, drivers, and newly designed or newly revamped automobiles.

The really serious business begins with the third race in South Africa. The Kyalami course outside Johannesburg presents a keen challenge and tends to sort out the year's best among men and machines.

Then the action proceeds to Europe. First there is Spain with its two tracks — one easy, one hair-raising — used on alternate years. Then on to Belgium, with the challenge of several different courses, some dangerously obsolete.

Towards the end of May, there is the Monaco Grand Prix. It is run through the streets of Monte Carlo — hazardous, colorful, glamorous, demanding split-second timing from drivers and perfect maneuverability of cars.

The summer continues with races in Sweden, the Netherlands, France, England, West Germany, Austria, and Italy.

Then the final act of the Grand Prix drama begins with a shift of scene. The racers fly off to North America for the Canadian Grand Prix in September. At the very end, there is the U.S. Grand Prix, held since 1961 at Watkins Glen, N.Y.

England's Graham Hill was World Champion Driver in 1962 and 1968.

Early daredevils line up for the start of the 1921 Grand Prix race at Le Mans, France.

Formula One

Early Grand Prix racing cars were nothing but souped-up touring machines. But enterprising builders (or "constructors," as they are elegantly known on the circuit) soon developed automobiles designed for racing and nothing else.

Engines quickly approached monster size, so in 1914 a restrictive "formula" was adopted in the interests of safety and sportsmanship. The formula, which has changed from time to time over the years, specifies the engine size and restricts weight and configuration as well.

The ultimate European racing machines are those in Formula I, the Grand Prix group. Formula I cars are single-seaters with lightweight, banana-shaped bodies and tiny, screamingly powerful engines. Tires are fat to get the best grip on the ground and improve cornering. In dry weather, the tires have no treads. If it rains (the race goes on, regardless) grooved tires are used.

Stabilizers are likely to sprout from the front and rear of a Formula I car. For awhile in the late 1960's, the cars even had wings! These were airfoils mounted on struts as much as 5 feet above the car. Airplane wings are designed to lift; but those on racing cars work in reverse, pressing the car down onto the road surface to improve traction. High-mounted wings were outlawed after the 1969 Spanish Grand Prix when two cars crashed after the wings fell apart.

Modern Grand Prix cars look fragile and dangerous, but they are tougher than they appear. The "monococque" bodies combine structural strength with light weight. In a crash, the frail suspension gives way and the wheels go flying; but the driver is usually safe.

The greatest danger to the Grand Prix driver is fire. Fuel tanks, consisting of rubber bags of gasoline, surround the cockpit of the car. If these rupture

in a crash, disaster may result. The latest cars have built-in fire-extinguishing equipment. Drivers wear flame-resistant coveralls and protective helmets; but sometimes, not even these are enough.

New Zealand's Denis Hulme speeds around the track at Watkins Glen.

The Old Champ's Nerve

Only 10 laps remained in the German Grand Prix of 1957. Leading the pack by 30 seconds was Juan Manuel Fangio of Argentina, four-time World Champion, who has been called the greatest Grand Prix driver of all time.

If the old champ could win this race, he would clinch his fifth championship. But the odds against him were overwhelming. His Maserati was forced to pit for fuel and new tires at this point in the race; while his rivals, driving newer, more efficient machines, could continue to the finish without a stop.

Fangio lost 52 seconds in the pit. Two English drivers in Ferraris, Peter Collins and Mike Hawthorn, whizzed past. How could Fangio overcome their lead in only 10 laps?

Fangio was 46 years old and overdue for retirement. Younger drivers whispered that he was over the hill. But as Fangio roared out of the pit onto the Nürburgring course, he determined to put on one last show.

Nürburgring is notorious for its 178 corners and its dangerous trees and ditches. Fangio cut those corners at unprecedented speeds and went airborne over bumps. Again and again he broke the lap-speed record, 9 minutes 28 seconds for 14.5 miles. The time gap slowly closed.

With two laps left, Fangio passed Collins. Then

he trailed Hawthorn through the tree-clad mountains toward the finish. As crowds in the grandstand howled, Fangio put on one last burst of speed and passed Hawthorn to win both race and championship. His last lap time was a fantastic 9 minutes 17 seconds. He had triumphed with 3 seconds to spare.

The great Juan Manuel Fangio races in 1954, breaking the Grand Prix Record with a speed of 125 mph.

Aussie Jack Pushes Home

The year was 1959, and Grand Prix racing was in the midst of a revolution. New little light-weight Cooper-Climax cars were challenging the heavier Ferraris, Maseratis, and BRM's — and winning.

Cooper's most successful driver was an Australian named Jack Brabham. In 1959, he started things right by winning the Monaco Grand Prix; but in the Dutch and French contests, more powerful cars won. Jack Brabham had earned 19 points toward the championship, however, with Tony Brooks second at 14.

In the British Grand Prix, Brabham nosed out his teammate, Bruce McLaren, by 0.2 second. The German contest was won by Tony Brooks. In the Portuguese Grand Prix (no longer run), Britisher Stirling Moss took first place and became Brabham's closest rival. The World Driving Championship would be decided at the U.S. Grand Prix, held for the first time in 1959.

The race took place at Sebring, Florida. Brooks fell out when his car was rapped. Moss led, but then his gear box failed.

That left Brabham with a comfortable lead. But nothing is ever certain in an automobile race! Just

The Belgian Grand Prix starts as drivers race to their cars.

one-third lap from the finish, Brabham's car ran out of gas and coasted to a stop. But Jack was game to the end. Three cars zoomed past Brabham as he *pushed* the dead Cooper-Climax over the finish line for a fourth-place finish amid delighted cheers. The 3 points thus earned gave Jack his championship, one of the strangest in Grand Prix history.

The Champion Who Never Was

After the mighty Juan Manuel Fangio retired in mid-1958, one man stood out among all the others on the Grand Prix circuit. He was Stirling Moss, a sports superstar to English racing fans during the 1950's and 60's despite the fact that he had never won the World Driving Championship!

He began competing in the earliest Coopers in 1948 when he was only 18, and gained fame as a driver of "British-style" cars — those scrawny, underpowered, little toys that were to revolutionize auto racing in decades to come.

Moss raced the British cars valiantly for years, losing the big races but gaining a reputation for driving skill and a stout heart. In 1954, he went foreign at last. The following year, he won the British Grand Prix — his first — in a Mercedes-Benz. He was runner-up driving champ that year and in the next three years also. His 1957 win in England was the first Grand Prix victory for a home-built car, a Vanwall.

His timing and his dashing manner became legendary. Having all the odds against him brought out his keenest will to win. In 1958, he won the Argentine Grand Prix in a tiny 170 bhp Cooper-

The French Grand Prix at Le Mans is the "grandfather" of all Grand Prix races.

Climax, defeating Ferraris and Maseratis with more than twice the horsepower.

His 16 Grand Prix victories are exceeded only by those of Fangio, Jimmy Clark, and Jackie Stewart. Yet Stirling Moss was ever an also-ran — the most acclaimed among Grand Prix drivers.

A Yank in the Grand Prix

He grew up a spoiled rich kid in California.

When he was 12, in 1939, his wealthy aunt bought him his first car; he learned to drive it in one day. Driving became his greatest pleasure, but he had no notions of going into racing until he began to go to college. There, bored with the dull business courses his family wanted him to take, young Phil Hill rebelled.

"I'm going to do something else," he declared So he became a sports-car racer. Later, he admitted it was a way of seeking public recognition aside from his family's status and wealth. This attitude is easily understood today; but in the late '40's and early '50's, Phil Hill was an oddball.

His greatest obstacle to success was his own nerves. He was a born worrier who suffered from ulcers brought on by the tension of racing. From time to time he had to drop out of the sports-car circuit in order to recover his health.

Despite his problems, however, he won major races in the United States, Sweden, Italy, Venezuela, Argentina, and at Nassau in the Bahamas. He set land-speed records at Bonneville Salt flats in Utah.

His favorite car was a Ferrari. The Italian company was impressed with Phil's driving and occasionally invited him to fill in on their team, which was the most highly regarded in all Europe. In 1957 Phil Hill was offered a permanent place on the

Phil Hill (14) gains on Count Wolfgang von Trips (16) in the French Grand Prix of 1958.

Ferrari team and proudly accepted.

He won the famous "24 Hours of Le Mans" in 1958 and was given a place on Ferrari's Formula I team, which was short-handed because of injuries and deaths. It was rare for an American to be accepted by European teams, but Phil Hill had paid his dues.

His first Grand Prix victory came in 1960 at Monza, Italy. Ironically, he beat out another Ameri-

can, Richie Ginther, who had been Phil's friend for years and who also drove for Ferrari.

But 1961 was to be Phil Hill's greatest year. He ran third in Monaco and second in Holland. In Belgium he dueled with teammate Count Wolfgang von Trips, got hit in the eye by a stone, but still won the race!

He spun out in France and earned no points, but in England he was second to von Trips. The two friends joked about their rivalry and wondered whether they would share the championship.

England's Grand Prix was won by Stirling Moss. Von Trips was second, and Phil Hill third. The German nobleman now led the championship scoring by 6 points. The Italian Grand Prix at Monza might decide it all.

It did, but not in a way Phil Hill expected. Wolfgang von Trips was recovering from a slow start when his Ferrari crashed a guardrail, and he was killed. Phil Hill went on to win the race and the championship.

At his friend's funeral, Phil Hill expressed the philosophy of many racing drivers when he said, "Everybody dies. Isn't it a fine thing that Trips died doing something he loved? I think he would rather be dead than not race."

Phil Hill wins at Le Mans.

Jim Clark, The Great One

He was a Scottish farmer's son, and the first thing on wheels that he loved was a tractor. When he was 9, he learned to drive his father's huge old car. With tiny Jim Clark at the wheel, the Alvis Speed 20 looked as though it was driving itself!

Jim didn't care for school work, so he was allowed to drop out at the age of 16 and go to work on the farm. A few sporty Jaguars raced around his neighborhood, but Jim Clark was more impressed by motorcycles. His parents said, "No." Motorcycles were too dangerous.

He had to stick to cars. Little by little he entered rallies and other auto sporting events in Scotland. The competition bug bit him; and he began to race in 1958, despite his family's objections. He had some success as a sports-car driver, attracting the attention of racer-turned-builder Colin Chapman. Chapman and other drivers praised Jim Clark's way with a wheel and convinced the young man that he could be both a farmer *and* a race driver if he really put his mind to it.

He began Grand Prix racing in 1960, first in Aston-Martins, and later in Colin Chapman's Lotus. By 1962 he was challenging the best drivers. He won his first Grand Prix race in Belgium that year, then took the British Grand Prix. This put him in a shared lead for the championship with Graham Hill. The two men diced for the World title until the very end of the Grand Prix circuit.

That year the South African Grand Prix was the last race. Jim was in the lead when a bolt in his engine worked loose, the oil leaked out, and he was finished.

Mechanical failure seemed to be the only thing that could stop Jim Clark in 1963. He won the Belgian, Dutch, French, British, Italian, Mexican, and South African Grands Prix! He lost at Monaco, Germany, and the United States when various car parts failed. Winning a record-smashing 7 out of 10 Grand Prix races made him a World Driving Champion of Champions.

In 1965, Jim Clark won his second World Championship after six Grand Prix victories. He also took his Lotus-Ford to the Indianapolis 500 and became the first non-American to win the classic race since 1916.

Not yet 30 years old, Clark seemed to become a better driver than ever as the years went by. He did not jump from team to team but stayed faithful to Lotus, a company which did not always have the fastest cars. By 1968 he had won 25 Formula I races, one more than the fabled Fangio, and seemed likely to go on forever.

He had won at South Africa. Then, in April he drove in a minor Formula II race in Germany where the track was slick with rain. He slid into a tree while going 150 miles an hour, and there was a fearful crash.

Jim Clark had written his life story some years earlier and had said, "You need more than your fair share of luck to make a successful career of motor racing."

But by April 7, 1968, Jim Clark had used his luck all up.

Dan Gurney's Eagle

The American who has won the most Grand Prix races is Dan Gurney.

After going to college and serving in the Army, Gurney became a foreman in an aluminum factory. He had not been trained as an engineer, but he showed a great natural aptitude for working with machinery.

In his spare time, Dan raced a Triumph TR2 sports car that he had bought used. Infected by the racing mania, he gave up his job to become a professional road-race driver. He progressed from California to Europe, where he joined the Ferrari group.

At first, he was a lowly test driver. By mid-1959, however, he was racing in Formula I. During the next five years, Gurney worked for several Grand Prix teams. He won the French Grand Prix in 1962 for Porsche and both the French and Mexican races in 1963 for Brabham-Climax.

Dan really longed to strike out on his own, building his own cars and fielding his own team. In 1966, he found backing, and All-American Racers was born.

Dan Gurney called his car the Eagle. Its Grand Prix triumph came in Belgium in 1967, when Dan won by the fastest average speed in Grand Prix history.

It takes enormous amounts of money to race on the Grand Prix circuit; and since Dan's outfit just couldn't stand the cost, he switched to American racing. Dan's Eagles came in first and second at Indy in 1968. (Dan drove the runner-up while Bobby Unser won.)

In 1970 Gurney retired from active racing to concentrate on building cars and managing his team.

Dan Gurney trails John Surtees of England and Lorenzo Bandini of Italy during the Monaco Grand Prix of 1967. Surtees was driving champion in 1964.

Jackie Stewart Wins It All

Today as TV cameras sweep in on a road race at Watkins Glen, Long Beach, or elsewhere, the voice you hear describing the action may have a Scottish burr. It it does, chances are the speaker is Jackie Stewart, three-time World Champion Driver and winner of 27 Grand Prix races.

Unlike many racers, Jackie Stewart chose to retire when he was at the height of his success. His reason was simple: he wished to go on living.

Jackie was born in Scotland, the son of a garage owner. He loved sports, especially fishing and trap-shooting. He left school to work in his father's garage and became a champion clay-pigeon potter. His older brother Jimmy was a sports-car racer, and it was natural that Jackie should drive the fast cars himself.

Between 1961 and 1964, he raced sports cars. The latter season saw him win 14 out of 16 races in a Formula III Cooper. He was as eager to graduate to Formula I as were the Grand Prix teams eager to sign him up. Jackie went to the BRM team and won the Italian Grand Prix in his rookie year, 1965.

Jackie Stewart in his Elf Team Tyrell races in the 1973 Grand Prix of Monaco.

Jackie Stewart always took a sane, careful approach to racing. Some Grand Prix drivers are described as "accidents waiting to happen," but never Jackie Stewart. He introduced the safety shoulder harness and was among the first drivers to wear flame-proof clothing.

Jackie won the 1966 Monaco Grand Prix for BRM, but then the team's cars fell below top-level

Monaco's Grand Prix is especially dangerous because it is run through streets in the heart of Monte Carlo. Jackie Stewart is at left, with Chris Amon coming up.

Stewart takes the checkered flag as he crosses the finish line in Monaco.

Grand Prix standards. Seeking a better ride, Stewart switched to the Tyrell team.

In 1968 despite a wrist injury, he won the Dutch, German, and U.S. races, almost grabbing the championship away from Graham Hill. The following season saw Jackie's plaid-banded helmet and blue Matra-Ford coming home first in 6 out of 11 Grand Prix contests.

Jackie Stewart was Champion Driver for the first time.

In 1970, Jackie got a new car — a March-Ford that give him a lot of trouble and allowed only a single win, in Spain. The Lord of Formula I that season was to be Jackie's closest friend in racing, Austrian Jochen Rindt. He won five times and had clinched the title when the circuit brought the drivers to Monza, in Italy.

There Jochen Rindt was killed in a practice run. Jackie was deeply shaken by his friend's death. For the first time, the World Championship of Driving was awarded posthumously.

In 1971, Jackie's Tyrell team had a new car — one with its own name on it. The American driver Mario Andretti won the opener at South Africa, but then Stewart won two in a row at Spain and Monaco. It rained in Holland, causing Jackie to spin and finish 11th. But he won the next three races in a row, as well as the Canadian Grand Prix, to take his second championship.

Mario Andretti of the United States leads the field in the 1971 South African Grand Prix. He won, only the fourth American ever to win a Grand Prix race.

BARDAHL

He was honored by Queen Elizabeth and earned nearly a million dollars. But a bad season lay ahead. In 1972 his car became balky and so did his health. He won four Grands Prix, but the championship went to Brazil's young Emerson Fittipaldi.

"I looked around and saw that I was no longer the young charger," Jackie said mournfully. He wondered what would happen to his family if he were killed. So he decided to retire after 1973, but he told no one of his decision.

Instead he went out and did his best with a car that was inferior to at least two of the 1973 contenders. Fittipaldi won in Brazil and Argentina. Then Jackie Stewart took the important South African Grand Prix. Fittipaldi conquered in Spain, but Jackie took three in a row at Monaco, Belgium and Holland. He would win once more, at the tricky Nürburgring in Germany, wrapping up his third World Championship of Driving.

At last he was free to retire with honor. His melancholy mood fell away as the world heaped glory upon him and congratulated him on his best season. Jackie Stewart smiled and laughed and felt very grateful.

He had beaten the fearful odds that threaten the life of even the best racing drivers.

He had gambled and won it all.

Emerson Fittipaldi signals his victory in the Argentine Grand Prix.

Showdown at Watkins Glen

Grand Prix racing is a new sport in the United States. Both the cars and the drivers for Formula I are derived from sports-car racing, and this kind of motor challenge has never been commonplace in America.

After World War II, increasing numbers of foreign-built sports cars were imported into the U.S. Their amateur drivers began racing them informally. In 1948, a "Grand Prix" sports-car race was organized in Watkins Glen, N.Y. It ballooned in popularity, and by 1951 it attracted over 100,000 people.

The Watkins Glen race was not sanctioned by the Federation Internationale de l'Automobile (FIA) which controls the Grand Prix circuit, but the FIA kept its eye on the growing road-race movement in America. By 1959, the United States was deemed "mature" enough to merit a genuine Formula I race of its own, but not at Watkins Glen.

Another, better-organized sports-car course was laid out at Sebring, Florida, in 1950. Sebring sportscar events were recognized by the FIA in 1953, and the governing body decided that Sebring should be the site of American Grand Prix contests.

The public, however, didn't agree. The first Grand Prix in 1959 was a financial disaster. The second, transferred to Riverside in California, didn't make much money either. The FIA gave a worldly sigh, and bowed to Watkins Glen.

A prototype Porsche sports car works out at the Sebring, Florida, track.

There the last Grand Prix of the year is held. Sometimes, as in 1974, that race decides the championship.

After Jackie Stewart retired in 1973, there was no clear-cut heir-apparent to the throne of World Champion Driver. The hottest contender was Brazilian Emerson Fittipaldi – who gained his reputation as the "Mr. Cool" of Grand Prix racing.

Fittipaldi started racing on a bicycle at the age of 5. He won trophies and graduated to motorcycles, then midget cars, then motor boats. Formula racing was the next step. Like most young drivers, Emerson broke in driving scaled-down versions of the Grand Prix challengers – Formula IV, III, and II cars – all more familiar to European racing fans than to Americans.

The big time came quickly to the talented Brazilian. By mid-season 1970, he was racing Formula I. He won his first Grand Prix at Watkins Glen that year and was appointed head driver for the Lotus team. At 24, he was the youngest man competing regularly on the Grand Prix circuit.

Despite his youth, Fittipaldi drove with a careful calculation that inspired the respect of the veterans. Lotus experimented with new automobiles during 1971, and Fittipaldi recorded no wins. In 1972, though, his JPS Ford 72D proved a perfect steed for a great driver. Emerson and the Ford won five races, including one brilliant duel with Jackie Stewart in England. At the season's end Emerson Fittipaldi was crowned World Champion, and South Americans cheered the successor to Juan Manuel Fangio.

Brazil's Fittipaldi rounds a curve on the Interlagos course at Sao Paulo, site of the 1974 Brazilian Grand Prix. He won.

The following year, of course, belonged to Jackie Stewart. Fittipaldi won three of the races, however; and when Stewart stepped down, the calm young Brazilian was ready.

It was a mixed-up season, 1974, with 14 races producing 7 different winners before the final showdown at Watkins Glen. Emerson Fittipaldi had won the Brazilian, Belgian, and Canadian Grand Prix. He was tied in points (52) with the Swiss driver Clay Regazzoni, who had won only the German race. An outside contender was Jody Scheckter of South Africa, a two-race winner with 45 points.

Perfect Indian Summer weather prevailed at Watkins Glen for the deciding Grand Prix. The little town in upstate New York was crowded with race buffs, international jet-setters, college students, and a group of freaky folk who camped in a swamp known as The Bog and held a weird festival all their own.

During the race itself, Emerson drove with caution. He knew that all he needed to win the championship was to beat Regazzoni and Scheckter. Fuel problems crushed the South African's hopes; then a broken suspension washed out Regazzoni. Cooly, Emerson Fittipaldi breezed home fourth, wrapping up his second world title amid the blazing autumn leaves of Watkins Glen.

Clay Regazzoni wins the 1975 Italian Grand Prix with an average speed of 218.034 kilometers per hour.

Agip
A112
128 3P
GOODYEAR
AUTOBIANCHI

The Grand Prix Challenge

The world of Grand Prix driving once included playboys and European noblemen. It was once the exclusive property of Europeans and snobbish international idlers known as "beautiful people." Lately, however, the Formula I races have a different look.

In 1975 the first woman driver, Lella Lombardi of Italy, took part in Grand Prix races. A strange, new 6-wheeled race car was unveiled. The city of Long Beach, California, put on an exciting "Formula 5000" event of its own, and was talked about as a new site for the World Championship races. Ordinary sports fans were beginning to sit up and take notice of the strange Grand Prix machines which had invaded American track racing and put a new kind of auto on the Yankee Championship Trail.

In 1975, the World Championship was won by Niki Lauda of Austria, who was victorious in five races, including Watkins Glen. The racing teams had money problems because of the world-wide recession, but the winners at the Glen split up a whopping $350,000 in prize money.

Even though the prize money dwindles, and the builders tighten their belts, Grand Prix racing will go on. The sport is perilous, and a race driver must give up hope of a normal life during the years of competition. But the Grand Prix challenge remains — and there will always be new young drivers eager to accept it.

Niki Lauda of Austria raises his hand to acknowledge cheers as he wins the 1975 World Driving Championship. At left is his teammate, Clay Regazzoni.

Graham Hill is chased by Sweden's Ronnie Peterson in the 1971 South African Grand Prix.

Grand Prix Formula 1 World Driving Champions

Year	Driver	Country	Car
1950	Nino Farina	Italy	Alfa Romeo
1951	Juan Manuel Fangio	Argentina	Alfa Romeo
1952	Alberto Ascari	Italy	Ferrari
1953	Alberto Ascari	Italy	Ferrari
1954	Juan Manuel Fangio	Argentina	Mercedes & Maserati
1955	Juan Manuel Fangio	Argentina	Mercedes
1956	Juan Manuel Fangio	Argentina	Lancia & Ferrari
1957	Juan Manuel Fangio	Argentina	Maserati
1958	Mike Hawthorn	England	Ferrari
1959	Jack Brabham	Australia	Cooper-Climax
1960	Jack Brabham	Australia	Cooper-Climax
1961	Phil Hill	U.S.A.	Ferrari
1962	Graham Hill	England	BRM
1963	Jim Clark	Scotland	Lotus-Climax
1964	John Surtees	England	Ferrari
1965	Jim Clark	Scotland	Lotus-Climax
1966	Jack Brabham	Australia	Brabham-Repco
1967	Denis Hulme	New Zealand	Brabham-Repco
1968	Graham Hill	England	Lotus-Ford
1969	Jackie Stewart	Scotland	Matra-Ford
1970	Jochen Rindt	Austria	Lotus-Ford
1971	Jackie Stewart	Scotland	Tyrell-Ford
1972	Emerson Fittipaldi	Brazil	JPS Ford 72D
1973	Jackie Stewart	Scotland	Tyrell-Ford
1974	Emerson Fittipaldi	Brazil	McLaren-Ford
1975	Niki Lauda	Austria	Ferrari

SPORTS CLASSICS

WORLD SERIES
U.S. OPEN GOLF CHAMPIONSHIP
WIMBLEDON TENNIS TOURNAMENT
KENTUCKY DERBY
INDIANAPOLIS 500
OLYMPIC GAMES
SUPER BOWL
MASTERS TOURNAMENT OF GOLF
STANLEY CUP
NBA PLAY-OFFS
ROSE BOWL
AMERICA'S CUP YACHT RACE
WINTER OLYMPICS
PGA CHAMPIONSHIP TOURNAMENT
TRIPLE CROWN
AMERICAN TENNIS CHAMPIONSHIP
DAYTONA 500
GRAND PRIX
BOXING'S HEAVYWEIGHT CHAMPIONSHIP

CREATIVE EDUCATION